Witness to History

The D-Day Landings

Sean Connolly

Heinemann Library
Chicago, Illinois

Designed by Heinemann Library
Produced for Heinemann by Discovery Books Ltd
Originated by Ambassador Litho Ltd
Printed and bound in China
by South China Printing

07 06 05 04 03
10 9 8 7 6 5 4 3 2 1

**Library of Congress Cataloging-in-Publication
Data**

Connolly, Sean, 1956-
    D-Day landings / Sean Connolly.
        p. cm. -- (Witness to history)
Summary: Discusses the events surrounding the D-
Day invasion of Europe
by Allied Forces on June 6, 1944, using primary
sources.
    ISBN 1-4034-4567-2 (HC) -- ISBN 1-4034-4575-3
(PB)
    1. World War, 1939-1945--Campaigns--France--
Normandy--Juvenile
literature. [1. World War, 1939-1945--Campaigns--
France--Normandy.] I.
Title. II. Witness to history (Heinemann Library
(Firm))
    D756.5.N6C66 2003
    940.54'21421--dc21
                                2003007108

Acknowledgments
The author and publishers are grateful to the
following for permission to reproduce copyright
material:

pp. 4, 7, 8, 17, 23, 38, 43, 50 Corbis; pp. 6, 22, 26
Popperfoto; pp. 9, 44, 46 Hulton-Deutsch
Collection/Corbis; pp. 10, 14, 28, 34, 42
Topham/Associated Press; pp. 12, 15, 16, 24, 25, 37
Topham Picturepoint; p. 18, 20 Topham/PA.; p. 19
Topham/ Photonews; p. 32 Associated Press; p. 36
Imperial War Museum; p. 40 Bettmann/Corbis; p. 45
Peter Newark's Military Pictures.

Cover photograph shows U.S. soldiers wading ashore
during the D-Day invasion of Normandy, France.
Reproduced with permission of Corbis.

The publishers would like to thank Bob Rees,
historian and teacher, for his assistance in the
preparation of this book.

Disclaimer
All Internet addresses (URLs) given in this book
were valid at the time of going to press. However,
due to the dynamic nature of the Internet, some
addresses may have changed, or sites may have
changed or ceased to exist since publication. While
the author and publisher regret any inconvenience
this may cause readers, no responsibility for any
such changes can be accepted by either the author
or the publisher.

Every effort has been made to contact copyright
holders of any material reproduced in this book. Any
omissions will be rectified in subsequent printings if
notice is given to the publishers.

Some words are shown in
bold, **like this.** You can find
out what they mean by looking
in the glossary.

Contents

Introduction

World War II was the deadliest conflict in history. It cost millions of lives, made millions more homeless, and left many countries crushed by its economic cost. For the countries that fought the war, far more was at stake than simply gaining or losing land. The war decided how people would live in the future: they would either be free to choose their own way of life or be forced to live under systems of government that disregarded many basic freedoms.

Military dictatorships

Although World War II was a global conflict, most of the fighting on land took place in Europe, North Africa, and the Asian countries bordering the Pacific Ocean. By the early 1930s, **military dictatorships** had gained power in Germany, Japan, and Italy. The leaders of these countries wanted to extend their power by invading neighboring territories. They formed an **alliance** and became known as the **Axis** powers. Germany's ruling **Nazi** Party, led by Adolf Hitler, believed that Germans were superior to other nationalities and therefore had the right to invade and occupy other countries.

Fighting the Axis powers were the **Allies,** led by Great Britain, the **Soviet Union,** and China. In 1941, the United States joined the Allies. These countries pledged to stop and reverse the advance of the Axis powers.

German troops march through the Arc de Triomphe into the heart of Paris, the capital city, after France surrendered on June 25, 1940.

The Axis countries made many advances in the first years of the war. Japan swept through much of south and southeast Asia, threatening India to the west and Australia to the south. By the time the United States joined the war in 1941, much of mainland Europe was under German control. Three million

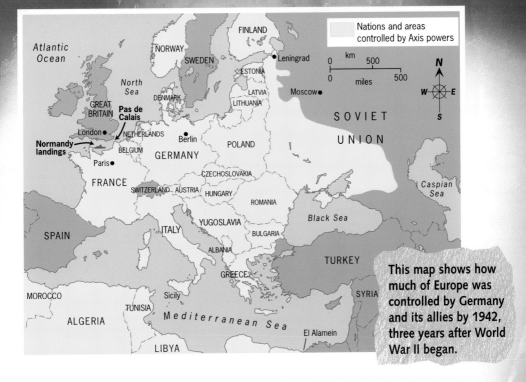

| | Nations and areas controlled by Axis powers |

This map shows how much of Europe was controlled by Germany and its allies by 1942, three years after World War II began.

German soldiers had entered the Soviet Union. The Soviet leader, Josef Stalin, insisted that Great Britain and the United States plan an attack against German-held France. This second **front,** he argued, would lessen the pressure on his own country. At a meeting in Tehran, in December 1943, the three major Allied leaders—Stalin, President Franklin Roosevelt, and British Prime Minister Winston Churchill—agreed that such an invasion should take place. However, a massive invasion force would be needed if the attack were to be successful.

D-Day and beyond

Early on June 6, 1944, a date now known as D-Day (which was the military's code name for the planned day of invasion), Allied planes began bombing the German coastal defenses. **Paratroopers** were dropped inland to cut off German supply routes. Soon after daybreak, troops began landing on five French beaches along the coastline of France's Normandy region. The fighting was fierce, but by the end of the day each one of the beaches was captured by the Allies. The Allies were then able to send more troops and equipment to France, using the captured beaches as ports. Over the next few weeks, the Germans were driven back from Normandy, although the fighting remained bitter. Nearly another year of war lay ahead, but now Germany was on the defensive. It would only be a matter of time before the Allies triumphed.

How Do We Know?

By studying history, we can learn about the events of the past. For example, if we need to find out about the fall of the Roman Empire or the Civil War, we can find many books and articles about these subjects. They can tell us when and how these events took place, as well as who the leading characters were. These sources often go on to explain not only why things have happened—by giving the background to the events—but also how the events themselves changed the course of history. Although these works are helpful and informative, they are often based on secondary sources, which are accounts that were written some time after the event and by people who were probably not personally involved.

Getting to the source

This book aims to use primary sources to tell the story of D-Day. These sources are the firsthand accounts written at the time by people who were involved in the events taking place. Historians dealing with events of long ago must rely on written primary sources such as codes of law, religious records, letters, and sometimes journals or diaries. But because D-Day is a more recent event, there are many people still alive who lived through this period. So, historians can use

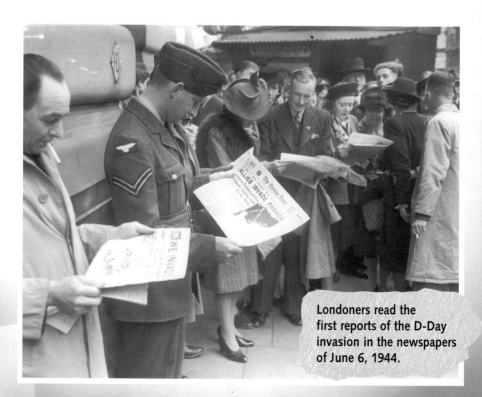

Londoners read the first reports of the D-Day invasion in the newspapers of June 6, 1944.

a much wider range of primary sources to get to the truth of this story. Tape recordings, online interviews, newspaper reports, and film footage of events add personal touches to the wealth of written material we have about this dramatic military victory. While looking at primary sources of this wartime era, historians must remember that **censorship** was imposed on reporting media, such as newspapers and radio. Even soldiers' letters sent home to their families were opened by censors, and any sensitive information was blacked out.

Putting it all together

Not every primary source is objective, and that is true of some of the sources you will find in this book. When historians are studying sources, they must be aware of the possible **bias** of writers, which can make some historical accounts unreliable. They have to compare accounts written by different people and

War reporters, such as the American Ernie Pyle, gave readers a firsthand account of the fighting in reports they sent home from the battlefield.

consider the possible **prejudices** the writers might have. For example, if the writer did not like Germans, he or she is less likely to give a completely truthful account of German victories and defeats. Furthermore, personal diaries and accounts tell the truth, but only as much as the writer can know. People in the thick of a battle can only observe what is happening around them, and they sometimes have no clear idea of which side is winning overall. On the other hand, we often know the outcome of a historical event, such as the D-Day invasion, but have little idea of what it was really like to live through it. The primary sources in this book provide a very personal and dramatic picture of one of the most important battles in history.

Early Planning

World War II began at different times for different nations. In China, war came in 1937 when the country was invaded by Japan. For the United States, the war did not start until 1941. However, many people think of the war as beginning in 1939 when **Nazi** Germany invaded and occupied Poland. By 1940, many countries—notably France, Belgium, Luxembourg, the Netherlands, Norway, and Denmark—had been defeated by, or had surrendered to, the Germans. Great Britain repelled the German advance during the Battle of Britain. This battle took place in 1940, when the British Royal Air Force narrowly defeated the German air force in the skies over southeast Britain. The German army remained in control of much of continental Europe, however, with troops and heavy **artillery** positioned along the northern coast of France within just a few miles of Britain. Then, in 1941, the Germans turned to the east, sweeping into the **Soviet Union** with tanks, planes, and more than 3 million soldiers. They raced to within 19 miles (30 kilometers) of the capital city, Moscow, and surrounded Russia's second most important city, Leningrad.

Great Britain, Germany's only remaining enemy in Western Europe, desperately needed a **strategy** to reverse this string of Nazi triumphs. The United States was not yet in the war. National pride, **morale,** and military sense demanded something big. In late 1941, the British chiefs of staff ordered Admiral Lord Louis Mountbatten to consider **amphibious** operations in German-controlled Europe.

An aircraft spotter scans the skies over London during the Battle of Britain in 1940. The Germans were trying to gain control of British airspace before launching an invasion of Britain.

Churchill's orders to Lord Mountbatten

In October 1941, British Prime Minister Winston Churchill summoned Lord Mountbatten back to London to take on a new position. Mountbatten, who had been waiting to take command of the aircraft carrier HMS *Illustrious* in the Pacific Ocean, was worried that he would be offered a boring desk job. Instead, Churchill had something far more dramatic in mind. Mountbatten recorded Churchill's words on October 22, 1941.

*You will carry on with the **commando** raids on the occupied coasts of Europe, not only to keep up our morale and to worry the Germans but because I want you to learn the technique of **opposed landings,** for you are to prepare for the invasion of Europe. We cannot win this war unless we land an army in France and defeat Hitler on land. You must arrange to collect soldiers, sailors, and airmen, put them in training-bases, teach them to operate as one force.*

*You must devise the new techniques, you must design new landing craft, new landing ships, the equipment, and the appliances necessary for invasion. The whole of the South of England is a **bastion** of defense against Hitler's invasion. You must turn that into a springboard for our own attack. Every other headquarters in England is thinking defensively, yours is to think only offensively.*

This photo of Admiral Lord Louis Mountbatten was taken in 1941, shortly after he was appointed Britain's chief of combined forces.

The U.S. Enters the War

On December 7, 1941, the Japanese bombed the American Pacific fleet moored at Pearl Harbor on the island of Oahu in Hawaii, thus bringing the United States into the war on the side of the **Allies.** The Pacific region immediately became an important area of fighting, but American forces also became involved in fighting the **Axis** powers in Europe and North Africa. Major-General Dwight Eisenhower was chosen as Supreme Allied Commander in 1942, but he soon found that the Americans and British disagreed about when and where to fight the Germans. Eisenhower and other senior Americans wanted to wait until 1943 and then attack German-controlled Europe directly. Senior British officials, believing that American forces lacked combat experience, wanted to attack a **flank** earlier, in 1942. The British already had some combat experience under the command of General Bernard Law Montgomery, who had won a victory against the Germans at El Alamein, Egypt, in October 1942.

In late 1942, Eisenhower led the Allies in Operation Torch in North Africa. It was the United States' first real land warfare experience against **Nazi** Germany. After a series of setbacks against the brilliant German General Erwin Rommel, the Allies drove the Germans out of North Africa in May 1943. Eisenhower was promoted to the rank of full general. Two months later, the Allies landed in Sicily and began a long and difficult campaign northward through Italy.

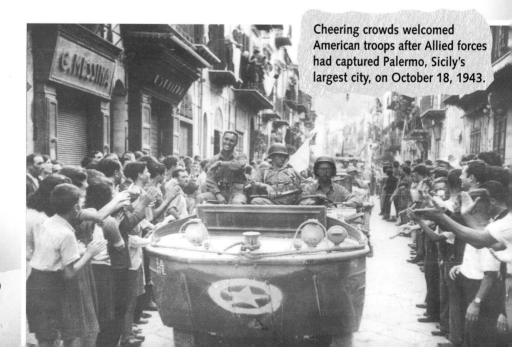

Cheering crowds welcomed American troops after Allied forces had captured Palermo, Sicily's largest city, on October 18, 1943.

Dean McCandless remembers his first days in occupied Sicily

Dean McCandless, an American **paratrooper,** was among the first Allied soldiers to set foot in Sicily. German forces were all around, but he managed to link up with other American soldiers. Many months of tough fighting lay ahead, but the experience would help Allied commanders plan the D-Day invasion less than a year later.

On the night of July 9, 1943, we jumped into Sicily. I landed near our intended drop zone, though we didn't know it at the time. Once out of my parachute, I soon located one of my men, Ott Carpenter, and we were joined by another half dozen troopers.

We went up the road until we ran into a machine-gun nest and scattered. Where everyone went, I'll never know but Ott and I remained together. Not knowing where we were, we decided to do what we had been instructed to do in that situation—head for the highest ground we could see. We . . . got to the top of a small mountain by dawn. . . .

When evening shadows began appearing, we began to work our way toward our own lines. It was near daybreak when I tripped over a gun muzzle extending out from some shrubs. . . . I jumped past it and shoved the muzzle of my rifle into the chest of a drowsy outpost soldier who shouted "God almighty don't shoot!" His southern drawl was music to our ears and the stress and tension of two nights and a day vanished.

Building Up a Force

With Americans fighting alongside the **Allies,** the war had entered a new phase and **morale** rose considerably. The United States had enormous industrial power, capable of producing large quantities of ships, weapons, and fuel. Its population of more than 130 million— almost three times that of Great Britain—provided many soldiers.

Throughout 1942, 1943, and 1944, **convoys** of American ships were sent to help the Allied cause in Europe. The destination for these troops and equipment was Great Britain. Some were sent on to North Africa and later Italy as part of Operation Husky, but many more remained in Great Britain. The British public largely welcomed the **GIs,** although some British men envied the Americans' better pay and equipment— and their popularity with British women! With all of these soldiers around, it was becoming obvious that the Americans and British, along with troops from other Allied countries, were preparing for a major operation. There was a sense of anticipation in the air, but the public had no idea of where or when such an operation would take place.

Private Gordon Carson recalls his excitement at being in wartime London

Private Gordon Carson was one of the thousands of American soldiers who arrived in Great Britain in the months leading up to the Normandy invasion. Like other Allied soldiers, he felt that he was part of a historic episode in world history. Here, he describes the sense of excitement and anticipation that filled the British capital city during the long buildup to the great invasion.

London to me was a magic carpet. Walk down any of its streets and every uniform of the Free World was to be seen. Their youth and vigor vibrated in every park and pub. To Piccadilly, Hyde Park, Leicester Square, Trafalgar Square, Victoria they came. The uniform of the Canadians, South Africans, Australians, New Zealanders, the Free French, Polish, Belgians, Dutch, and of course the English and Americans were everywhere. Those days were not lost on me because even at twenty years of age, I knew I was seeing and being a part of something that was never to be again. Wartime London was its own world.

Huge arrays of field guns and other military equipment were stored at secret locations across the British countryside during the buildup to the D-Day invasion.

A Solemn Promise

The leaders of the three major **Allied** powers—Franklin Roosevelt, Winston Churchill, and Josef Stalin—met for four days at the end of 1943 in Tehran, the capital of Iran. They wanted to decide on a **strategy** for fighting the **Axis** powers in Europe. Everyone agreed that an attack needed to be made, but the question was where and when. Stalin believed that his country, the **Soviet Union,** had been bearing an overwhelming share of the Allied defense against Hitler. The average number of Soviet soldiers and citizens dying every day, trying to defeat the Germans, was around 19,000. (At that rate, 20 million Soviet citizens and soldiers perished by the end of the conflict.) Stalin therefore insisted on a second **front**—a full-scale Allied assault on Western Europe.

By late 1943, when the three main Allied leaders met in Tehran, German troops had captured large parts of the western Soviet Union.

The result of the conference was a spirited statement of the determination and unity of the Allies. It was agreed that the invasion of Europe should take place during May 1944 and that the Soviets would launch an attack at the same time to prevent the Germans from moving their forces away from the **Eastern Front.** Behind the scenes though, Roosevelt and Churchill knew that they had to come up with an invasion plan. Within days General Dwight Eisenhower was made Supreme Commander of the Allied Expeditionary Force in Europe. He would be responsible for uniting the commanders of several nations and mounting a full-scale invasion of Western Europe. The invasion was given the code name Operation Overlord.

Declaration of the three powers

The official statement at the end of the four-day Allied conference in Tehran masked most of the tension and disagreements of the meeting. The leaders knew the importance of building **morale** among troops. The rousing words of December 1, 1943, were intended to raise their confidence and send a clear signal to Germany that the Allies were united.

We the President of the United States, the Prime Minister of Great Britain, and the Premier of the Soviet Union, have met these four days past, in this, the Capital of our Ally, Iran, and have shaped and confirmed our common policy.

We express our determination that our nations shall work together in war and in the peace that will follow.

As to war—our military staffs have joined in our round table discussions, and we have concerted our plans for the destruction of the German forces. We have reached complete agreement as to the scope and timing of the operations to be undertaken from the east, west, and south.

The common understanding which we have here reached guarantees that victory will be ours. . . . No power on earth can prevent our destroying the German armies by land, their U Boats [submarines] by sea, and their war planes from the air. . . . Our attack will be relentless and increasing. . . .

We came here with hope and determination. We leave here, friends in fact, in spirit, and in purpose.

ROOSEVELT, CHURCHILL and STALIN

Signed at Tehran, December 1, 1943

Hitler's Role

Germany's military leaders knew that it was only a matter of time before the **Allies** launched some sort of major attack from Britain, aimed at coastal France. But the questions remained: where in France would the attack be, and how should Germany prepare for it? The German leaders believed that the attack would come from across the Pas de Calais (map page 5) because the English Channel is at its narrowest there. Naturally, the Germans had this area heavily defended. The alternative invasion site was Normandy, which was less defended. From the Allied viewpoint, Normandy—with its broad, sandy beaches—was ideal for landing a large invasion force, and the port of Cherbourg could be used to bring in supplies (map page 30).

Erwin Rommel (left) and Gerd von Rundstedt were in charge of German military preparations for the expected Allied attack on German-held France in 1944.

Gerd von Rundstedt, overall commander of Germany's forces on the **Western Front,** believed that it would be impossible to set up powerful forces along all of the 2,500-mile (4,000-kilometer) French coastline. He preferred to keep most of Germany's forces inland, near Paris, ready to move quickly to whichever spot the Allies chose to invade. Erwin Rommel, commander of Germany's forces in northern France and Belgium, disagreed. He believed that most of Germany's troops and equipment should be lined up along the coast, behind the **artillery** posts, machine-gun nests, and other defensive structures known as the Atlantic Wall.

Both leaders knew that Germany could choose only one of these approaches because so many German soldiers were already fighting against **Soviet** troops on the **Eastern Front.** The ultimate choice belonged to the German leader Adolf Hitler, who often issued orders that showed he had no real understanding of the problems involved.

Guenther Blumentritt's memoirs

Guenther Blumentritt, von Rundstedt's chief of staff, was aware of the disagreement between his own superior and Rommel over how to prepare for an Allied attack. His **memoirs** describe their differing approaches and the role played by Adolf Hitler himself in the planning.

Hitler agreed in general with both these reports. . . . To be sure, he held fast to the immediate defense of the coast in the Rommel sense, but agreed to the formation of Western Command reserves around Paris. But these—since fresh divisions were no longer available—were to consist of **panzer** divisions from the east in need of overhaul. . . . Hitler's tendency to overrate the value of the defense systems and fortifications . . . was generally known. He believed, or imagined, that a blue line along the coast with lots of fortifications . . . would completely seal off any attacker. **Illusory** planning maps were contemplated on the map table! They have a calming effect on those with a flair for fantasy. But such people would have been unpleasantly surprised could they have seen on the spot how poor and thin this **"garrison"** really was. Hitler's preference for steel, concrete, and iron, and the growing anxiety over the offensive that was being prepared by the Allies . . . led him to dream of banishing misfortune by pure defense.

Adolf Hitler, known as **"der Führer"** (the Leader), commanded complete obedience from the German people, including Germany's military leaders.

17

A Phantom Army

One of the most important **Allied** weapons in the buildup to D-Day was **intelligence**. Members of the French **Resistance** risked their lives to send information about German military preparations to Allied headquarters. They also destroyed bridges and railway lines that the Germans needed to send supplies of ammunition to the coast. A crucial breakthrough came when the British cracked the secret code that the Germans used for all of their messages. The British code-breaking operation, known as Ultra, provided the Allies with the latest information about where and when the Germans would move troops and equipment.

The next step was to trick the Germans about the nature of the invasion itself. The Allies knew

Brenda Webb describes how codes were cracked at Bletchley Park

The British Navy captured a German Enigma code-making machine in 1941. The codes were supposedly unbreakable, but top mathematicians working at Bletchley Park, north of London, eventually cracked the codes. Eighteen-year-old Brenda Webb was part of the top-secret British intelligence that helped decode many German messages.

that the Germans expected the attack to come across the Pas de Calais. They decided to play on this mistaken belief by setting up a nonexistent army in southeast England in early 1944. George Patton, one of the most famous American generals, was given command of this phantom army. Fake army camps, built from canvas and plywood, sprang up in this area, along with inflatable tanks and mock ships. Deliberately false radio messages, which the Allies knew the Germans would overhear, added to the deception. And thanks to the Ultra system, the Allies knew their trick was working.

Germany's Enigma code-making machine looked like a typewriter, but messages typed into it could be jumbled to make them difficult for the Allies to understand.

We were told never ever to tell anyone about it, not your boyfriend, parents, anyone. . . . With Enigma, any message could be easily translated into groups of five letters, transmitted in **Morse code** and then decoded by the machine using the same settings. The difficulty of the task facing us can be gauged from the number of settings for an Enigma machine—150 million million million.

Good intelligence work, educated guesses, and mind-numbing thoroughness, combined with sloppy German operators, meant signals could be decoded in days or hours.

Much of it depended on the mathematical probability of a particular letter occurring, so machines were built enabling **decryption** that took days manually to be done in half an hour. In fact, they developed the world's first programmable computer, but like everything at Bletchley, it remained a secret and its designers, notably mathematician Alan Turing, never received credit for their work.

The peace and quiet of Bletchley Park, a country house north of London, provided an ideal setting for British experts trying to discover the secrets of Germany's Enigma code-making system.

The Pressure Builds

The buildup to D-Day was incredibly complicated, involving hundreds of aircraft, some 5,000 ships, and more than 170,000 soldiers. It all had to go like clockwork. The invasion forces had to sweep across the English Channel from southern England and overwhelm German positions in coastal France with perfect timing. By the spring of 1944, **Allied commandos** had made many secret missions to Normandy to inspect the invasion beaches and to check on German defenses.

Meanwhile, troops stationed in England began to rehearse their roles in a series of drills and dry runs. Secrecy was to be maintained at all times, and **civilians** living in the southern counties often came across notices outside troop camps that read "DO NOT TALK TO THE TROOPS." In April 1944, one of these rehearsals ended tragically when some landing ships ran into German E-Boats (small, fast torpedo boats) and two vessels were sunk, killing 639 American soldiers. Exercise Eagle, the American 101st Airborne Division's rehearsal for the whole operation, took place from May 9 through May 12, 1944, less than a month before the scheduled attack. It involved rehearsals of **paratroop** drops—one of the key elements of the planned invasion. Some parts of this rehearsal failed miserably when troops were separated from each other and landed nowhere near their planned meeting points. Although most of this and other Allied exercises did go according to plan, the soldiers began to realize that there would be no room for error when the real invasion took place.

The Slapton Sands dry run for the Normandy invasion turned into a disaster. Due to a series of mistakes, more than 700 people died in several incidents in which soldiers were drowned, accidentally shot, or hit by rocket fire.

Alan Moorehead writes

Alan Moorehead, an Australian living in Great Britain, became a war correspondent for the *Daily Express* newspaper. Unlike the soldiers he followed across the English Channel on D-Day, he was able to go where he chose, gathering information to send back to Great Britain. Immediately after the war, he wrote a book about his experiences. This excerpt shows the mood in Great Britain shortly before the landings took place.

The waiting in Britain had gone on so long. The mystery and secrecy of the operation made it more difficult. Although there was a general certainty that the landing would occur, people were without the technical knowledge of how it would be done. . . . All that one could see ahead was a deliberately planned massacre. It would have been much easier if they could have watched the preparations; the submarines stealing in to chart the coast and the seabed; the commandos landing on the beaches to gather information; the hundreds of boats collecting in the ports; the five thousand aircraft preparing for the day. . . .

A dead, heavy mood settled over the country, and this was communicated to the army. Having prepared so long, so thoroughly . . . it seemed on some black days that one thing would be lacking—the spirit to put the plan into operation. . . . May turned into June. Surely it could not be much longer now. Standing on the South Downs one could see the English Channel, bright and clear and calm. It was hot . . . the country never looked more calm and beautiful.

The Strain of Command

The tensions and concerns present during the buildup to D-Day affected everyone involved with the operation. The man in charge of the entire operation—General Dwight D. Eisenhower, known by his nickname "Ike"—was a popular leader with his soldiers and impressed the British with his combination of friendly charm and decisiveness. With his quick smile and easy-going manner, he seemed to typify the values that the **Allies** were fighting to preserve: friendship, compassion, and loyalty.

Behind the scenes, though, Eisenhower was feeling the strain. He smoked heavily and found it hard to sleep. The news about the German defenses along the French coast made planning complicated. The Germans had installed metal stakes and other obstacles to block the landing of Allied boats and equipment. These were just under water, and impossible to see at high tide. If the attack came at low tide, however, thousands of Allied soldiers would be sitting targets for German machine guns. Eisenhower knew that the invasion force needed to land at **half tide.** The timing of the invasion had become even more critical.

Eisenhower found that he sometimes had to **reprimand** his own generals. General George Patton, who had proved himself to be a successful and popular leader, already had an unfriendly relationship with General Montgomery. The success of the invasion depended on good relations between Britain and the U.S., especially at the highest level. Eisenhower could not risk endangering this precious relationship.

General Montgomery (in front), commander of Britain's forces in Western Europe, and General Dwight Eisenhower (to Montgomery's right), Supreme Allied Commander, oversee British-American preparations in early 1944.

General Eisenhower's letter to General George Patton

In April 1944, General Patton offended the British with some remarks he made near his base in Cheshire, England. Here is an extract from the letter Eisenhower sent to him on April 29, 1944.

I have warned you time and again against your **impulsiveness** and have flatly instructed you to say nothing that could possibly be misinterpreted. You first came into my command at my own insistence because I believed in your fighting qualities and your ability to lead troops in battle. At the same time I have always been fully aware of your habit of dramatizing yourself and of committing **indiscretions** for no other apparent purpose than of calling attention to yourself. I am thoroughly weary of your failure to control your tongue and have begun to doubt your all-around judgment, so essential in high military position. My decision in the present case will not become final until I have heard from the **War Department.** I want to tell you officially and definitely that if you are again guilty of any indiscretion in speech or action, I will relieve you instantly from command.

General Patton was a clever but hot-headed soldier whose remarks offended the British. Nevertheless, he played an important role in directing American troops in Normandy in 1944.

German Preparations

Although the **Allies** had superior air power and an element of surprise in choosing exactly where the attack would take place, the Germans had other advantages. Even in 1944, German war defenses were very strong. They had weapons that were as good as, if not better than, those of the Allies. No one could question the fact that Germany had successful and experienced soldiers. Another advantage for the Germans was their control of land communications—trains and trucks (though they still also relied on horses). These vehicles could carry troops and equipment far more easily than ships. Despite some disagreements about how best to defend against the Allied attack, the Germans had a large workforce to carry out their plans.

Starting in 1942, prisoners from Germany's European victories were put to work building a line of forts and areas for guns—about 2,400 miles (3,800 kilometers) long—along the west coast of France. The Germans called this line of defense the Atlantic Wall. Its job was to drive back Allied invaders on the beaches, making it impossible for them to gain a foothold on the continent. Armored units, using Germany's feared Panther and Tiger **panzers,** could rush to back up any part of the wall that faced Allied attack. Hitler had once boasted that this defense line was "**impregnable** against every enemy." However, as the success of the Allied landings was to show, his confidence in the wall defenses was misplaced.

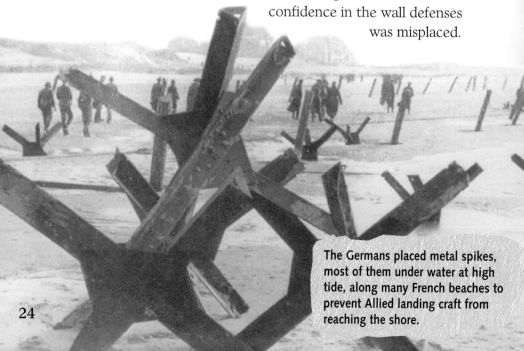

The Germans placed metal spikes, most of them under water at high tide, along many French beaches to prevent Allied landing craft from reaching the shore.

Major Hans von Luck's memoirs

In May 1944, Major Hans von Luck was given command of a panzer regiment based near the city of Caen, Normandy. In this extract from his **memoirs,** Luck reports the welcome he received from General Edgar Feuchtinger, his superior officer in the region.

Our division is the only one near the coast behind the Atlantic Wall, which, here in Normandy, is not yet fully developed and manned by an inexperienced **infantry** division. The anticipated Allied landing is not expected in Normandy, but rather in the Pas de Calais, the shortest distance between England and the Continent. But Caen, as an important industrial city, is also a key point. That is why it was decided to move a panzer division here by the Atlantic Wall. All the same, we have to reckon on airborne landings or large-scale **commando** operations, which would serve as a diversion from the actual landing. For that reason, Rommel considers it very important that the division should take up combat positions even in the hinterland [land lying behind a coastal region].

Our division has strict orders not to intervene in the event of enemy landings until cleared by Army Group B. Rommel wants all units to make themselves familiar with the terrain—also by night—and regular combat exercises to be carried out. I hope, my dear Luck, that you will be happy with us and I wish you lots of luck.

Huge guns, protected in concrete **bunkers,** formed the backbone of Germany's Atlantic Wall defense against the expected Allied invasion.

"OK, Let's Go"

Tides and ocean currents played a huge part in the scheduling of the D-Day attack. The biggest concern was the weather. The target date was June 5, but the weather deteriorated as the day approached. Would the planes be able to fly? Would all of the soldiers become seasick before even landing? Would gales blow landing craft back out to sea, or even sink them? These were some of the most pressing concerns as the date grew nearer. However, there would be an almost unbearable two-week wait if the attack was delayed by more than a day.

Senior **Allied** generals and admirals decided to wait an extra day and then discuss whether to go ahead with the invasion. In the early hours of June 5, 1944, they met again. The wind blew sheets of rain against the windows while **meteorologist** J. M. Stagg announced that the weather would improve briefly on June 6. Eisenhower then took a poll among those present. Opinion was divided, so the decision rested on Eisenhower's shoulders. He decided that the landings would go ahead, on the morning of June 6, 1944. "OK, let's go" were Ike's words at 4 A.M. on June 5, 1944. They set in motion the greatest military attack in history. There would be no turning back.

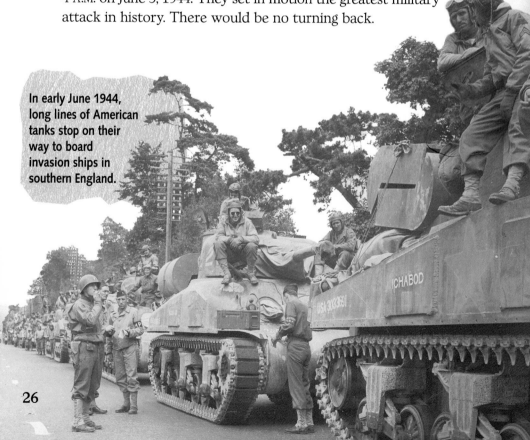

In early June 1944, long lines of American tanks stop on their way to board invasion ships in southern England.

Eisenhower's orders to the soldiers

General Eisenhower composed a stirring Order of the Day, which was distributed to each soldier taking part in Operation Overlord on June 6, 1944. In it, he summed up the hopes of everyone who prayed for the defeat of Hitler's **Nazi** government.

Soldiers, Sailors, and Airmen of the Allied Expeditionary Forces: You are about to embark upon the Great Crusade, toward which we have striven these many months. The eyes of the world are upon you. The hopes and prayers of liberty-loving people everywhere march with you. In company with our brave Allies and brothers-in-arms on other **Fronts** you will bring about the destruction of the German war machine, the elimination of Nazi **tyranny** over **oppressed** peoples of Europe, and security for ourselves in a free world.

Your task will not be an easy one. Your enemy is well trained, well equipped, and battle-hardened. He will fight savagely.

But this is the year 1944! Much has happened since the Nazi triumphs of 1940-1941. The United Nations have inflicted upon the Germans great defeats, in open battle, man-to-man. Our air offensive has seriously reduced their strength in the air and their capacity to wage war on the ground. Our Home Fronts have given us an overwhelming superiority in weapons and **munitions** of war, and placed at our disposal great reserves of trained fighting men. The tide has turned! The free men of the world are marching together to Victory!

I have full confidence in your courage, devotion to duty, and skill in battle. We will accept nothing less than full victory!

Good Luck! And let us all beseech the blessing of Almighty God upon this great and noble undertaking.

Seeing Them Off

The departure of the D-Day invasion force was dramatic. On June 5, thousands of **Allied** ships of all kinds, including battleships, cruisers, **minesweepers,** landing craft, hospital ships, and ammunition ships, gathered in the blustery waters of the English Channel. That night hundreds of planes—carrying over twenty thousand **paratroopers**— thundered overhead, all heading to the south. The months of planning, all of the drills and exercises, were over. In order to reach the French coast by the early morning **half tide,** all of the troop ships had to leave English ports under cover of darkness. The largest invasion in history had begun.

The British public, especially those living in southern England where most of the troops had been stationed, knew that a historic moment had arrived. Even the foreign troops who had been training in England—the Americans, Canadians, South Africans, and other Allies—had become part of the English social scene. The number of American soldiers based in Britain had doubled in the first six months of 1944, rising from 774,000 at the beginning of the year to 1,537,000 in the week preceding the final assault. Now many of them had gone, and some people wondered when, or if, they would ever see them again.

Landing craft carrying British Royal Marines gather in the English Channel on the evening of June 5, 1944, before taking part in the D-Day landings.

An English housewife remembers

Weymouth was one of the southern English ports that acted as a launch pad for the Allied invasion. In this extract, a Weymouth housewife describes her sudden sense of loss when she noticed the empty harbor on the morning of June 6, 1944. The invasion force had left in the night.

That Tuesday morning—the 6th—I remember looking out to sea to the spot that the Yanks called "Piccadilly Corner" because it was there that the landing craft always congregated on the training exercises. And it was empty. For the first time in six months I couldn't see a ship, where there had always been scores of them. They'd gone, the Yanks, and we knew where. I thought of my friend Al who was with the American 1st **Infantry** Division and wondered at that moment where he was now and how he was getting on and whether I'd ever see him again. Then . . . I spotted one of those daft [silly] little signs that the Yanks chalked up everywhere that year. . . . It was a drawing of a fat-nosed, stupid-looking chap peering over a wall with the words printed below, KILROY WUZ HERE. I don't know what it was supposed to mean and have never found out. But at that moment it got me. I wasn't very flighty or particularly silly in those days, but for me it seemed to say that my Al had come and gone and like the rest of the Yanks, wouldn't come back. Kilroy wuz here, I thought, and burst into tears.

In the Air

General Eisenhower was sure that the superiority of **Allied** airpower would be unquestionable in Operation Overlord. This advantage had already helped prepare the way for the invasion. British and American planes had prevented German reconnaissance aircraft (spy planes) from getting a true picture of the preparations in southern England. They had also destroyed many transportation routes and strongholds in France before the attack took place. Information sent by the French **Resistance** greatly aided British and American air crews in targeting their attacks.

Now, with the attack under way, the air crews knew that their job was to help the massive troop and equipment landings at five Normandy beaches, code-named Juno, Gold, Sword, Utah, and Omaha. British troops landed at Sword and Gold, and Canadian troops landed at Juno; troops from these three beaches were expected to join together soon after the landing. Americans were landing at Utah and Omaha. Planes dropped thousands of **paratroopers** beyond the German coastal defenses. Others towed gliders carrying guns and vehicles and sent them on their way to the same destination. Still others continued their preinvasion job of pounding the German **artillery** posts with powerful bombs. On the same night, the French Resistance carried out over 1,000 **sabotage** attacks against railroads and other lines of communication in German-held France.

Southampton
Portsmouth
Brighton
Bournemouth
Weymouth
Isle of Wight

N
W—E
S

ENGLISH CHANNEL

Utah
Omaha
Gold
Juno
Sword

INVASION BEACHES

Cherbourg
Le Havre
Bayeux
Caen
St-Lô
Falaise
Avranches
Orne River

0   km   50
0   miles   50

This map shows part of the northern coastline of France and the position of the Normandy beaches where the D-Day landings took place.

James Delong remembers his first mission of the D-Day operation

James Delong was a crew member of an American B-26 bomber which attacked German coastal artillery sites in the hours before the D-Day landings. His crew had already flown fifty-five missions over Europe, but the early morning of June 6, 1944, was the first time they would take off in darkness.

On June 6, we woke at 01.30. We knew that this was the day; this was the hour we had been waiting for. . . . Boy, it's dark and rainy. We're not accustomed to this at all; we've done only daylight missions. Time to fire the engines. . . . We have a climb pattern, but no time for practice. It's got to be perfect the first time. Throttles wide open, and off we go. . . . The sky was full of planes, and below, the water was covered with surface vessels. We expected to see German fighters as we neared the coast, but didn't. As we approached the target, the bomb-bay doors opened and "Bombs away!" There was light **flak** coming up, and the bombardier said we got a good hit. Out over the French countryside, scattered everywhere, were parachutes and pieces of huge crashed gliders. I don't believe I saw an undamaged one. I had this sick feeling that things were not going well.

We made a sweeping turn back to the coast and the formation tightened, and I could see aircraft everywhere approaching the coast. We flew back over the sea full of vessels and made landfall over the white cliffs at Beachy Head [on the British Coast], and then around the London balloons to our base. We made another flight later in the day.

The First Fighting

Allied aircraft flew over the Normandy coast in the early hours of June 6, 1944. Once past the German coastal defenses, they dropped thousands of **paratroopers** who had an important role to play if the invasion was to be a success. These men had to capture bridges, railway lines, and roads that the Germans would use for communication and reinforcements once the Allied landing force reached the beaches.

Parachute training was difficult and intense. The men knew that they ran a high risk of being killed or captured once the operation began. Some of the paratroopers were shot while floating down; others got tangled in trees or wires. Still others landed safely, but well away from their intended targets—and from their fellow soldiers. Despite these difficulties, the Allied paratroopers did gain control of many roads and railway lines. The American 82nd Division secured an important road junction at Sainte Mere Eglise (between Utah and Omaha Beaches). The British captured the Merville **Battery,** near the mouth of the Orne River (map page 30). These early successes were vital, preventing German tanks positioned at Caen from moving east and crushing the invasion before the troops could get off the beaches. For the first time in four years, Allied soldiers were fighting the Germans on French soil. The battle had begun.

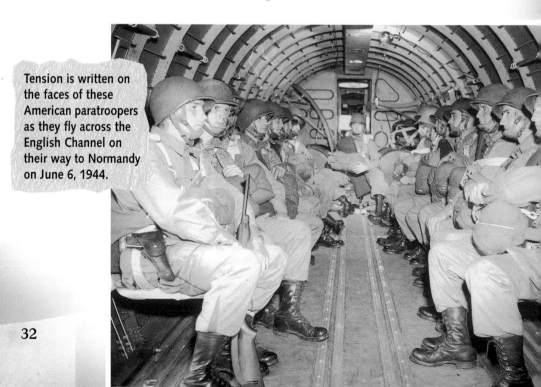

Tension is written on the faces of these American paratroopers as they fly across the English Channel on their way to Normandy on June 6, 1944.

Sergeant Thornton fires an important shot

Sergeant "Wagger" Thornton was a member of the British 6th Airborne Division, which landed by the Orne River in Normandy on June 6. They encountered fierce German resistance after they had captured the vital Pegasus Bridge over the river. The PIAT (an anti-tank grenade launcher) shot that he describes here was the most important shot in this particular fight, as it forced German troops to retreat and prevented tanks from stopping the Sword Beach landings.

The tanks were making their way down, probably to recapture the bridge, and Howard asked Fox if he had a PIAT, and I suddenly found myself entrusted with the PIAT. I took a chap with me, to be a number 2, and off we went.

Now a PIAT is a load of rubbish [garbage] really. First, you're a dead loss if you have to go even 50 yards, and second, you must never, never miss. If you do, you've had it, because by the time you reload the thing and cock it, which is a chore on its own, everything is gone. You're **indoctrinated** into your brain that you mustn't miss. So, I lay down with this other guy about 30 yards from the T-junction of the road. I was shaking like a leaf. Sure enough, in about three minutes this tank appears, the old wheels were rattling away, and I could more hear it than see it. I took aim, and although shaking, bang, and off it went. The thing exploded right bang in the middle, and a couple of minutes later, all hell let loose. I was so excited and shaking, and I had to move back a bit. Two or three guys jumped out of the thing, and I said to my number 2 to give them a few bursts from the Sten [machine gun], which he did.

The German Response

All through the beginning of 1944, while the **Allied** invasion force had been preparing for the D-Day landings, the German forces that were lined up along the French coast had been going through their own drills and exercises. Each soldier knew exactly what he needed to do—and where he needed to be—when the invaders arrived.

As Allied planes began their bombing runs over Normandy before dawn on June 6, 1944, however, the Germans were shocked. The troops stationed there, like nearly all Germans, had expected that the invasion would take place farther to the north, near Calais. While the bombs rained down on the Normandy stretch of Germany's Atlantic Wall, the Germans began getting reports of **paratroopers** landing farther inland. Their months of preparation would now need to be put into practice, but the massive air attack warned them of the hard fighting that lay ahead.

While some of the German troops stationed along the Atlantic Wall were well trained and well equipped, others were poorly equipped and undermanned. As became clear when the Allies began to round up prisoners, many of the German troops were very young—only sixteen or seventeen years old. Some were not even German, but had been **conscripted** into the army from the German-occupied territories in Eastern Europe and the **Soviet Union.**

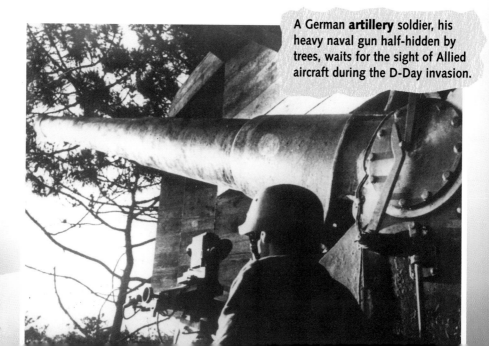

A German **artillery** soldier, his heavy naval gun half-hidden by trees, waits for the sight of Allied aircraft during the D-Day invasion.

Franz Gockel remembers his feelings of surprise when the Allied bombers appeared

Franz Gockel was a German **infantry** soldier stationed along the coast behind Omaha Beach. Like most other German soldiers along this stretch of French coastline, he had expected the Allied landing for months. However, the attack was still a surprise when it took place on June 6, 1944. Gockel soon realized that Allied air power would win the day.

The alarm call into the **bunker** woke us from a deep sleep. . . . We had so often been shaken to our feet by this call in the past weeks that we no longer took the alarms seriously, and some of the men rolled over in their bunks and attempted to sleep. An **NCO** brought us to our feet with the words "Guys, this time it's for real. They're coming!"

We sprang into action . . . and ran to our positions. Our coastal section remained quiet—nothing moved. Was it once again a false alarm? The silence weighed heavily upon us and the tension continued to build. Soon the sound of bomber squadrons could be detected in the distance. With the morning dawn came more bombers. . . .

The bombers were suddenly over us and it was too late to spring into the prepared dugout for cover. I dived under the gun as bombs screamed and hissed into the sand and earth. Two heavy bombs fell on our position. Debris and clouds of smoke enveloped us; the earth shook; eyes and nose were filled with dirt, and sand ground between teeth. There was no hope for help. No German aircraft appeared, and this sector had no **antiaircraft** guns.

Beach Combat

The main fighting on D-Day came along the five invasion beaches. Troop ships, along with open-topped, flat-bottomed LCIs (Landing Craft **Infantry**) and LSTs (Landing Ship Tank), carried the soldiers across the English Channel. The LCIs, the LSTs, and the other smaller landing craft then made the dangerous last leg of the journey into the shallow waters close to the beaches, where the soldiers jumped out to wade ashore.

Many British soldiers arrived on the Normandy beaches with bicycles to help them move more quickly once they reached the shore.

Death and destruction seemed to engulf the **Allied** troops. Their vessels bobbed and swayed in the waves, causing many men to be seasick. Many U.S. troops landing at Utah Beach were slumped down vomiting—or already dead from machine-gun fire—as their landing craft opened their hatches. They were also in the line of German fire from machine guns and heavier **artillery.** Canadians landing at Juno Beach could see Germans perched in church steeples and other tall buildings, signalling the Allied positions to machine gunners on the ground. The British 3rd Division, landing at Sword, found themselves facing a German tank division. It was up to the Allied soldiers to take cover from this fire wherever they could find it: behind sand dunes, broken equipment, or even behind the bodies of fallen soldiers.

J.H. Hamilton, a Canadian soldier, remembers

J.H. Hamilton, a Canadian soldier in the Royal Winnipeg Rifles, landed at Juno Beach in the main D-Day invasion. His landing craft lost an engine on the way, leaving the men open to German fire for far longer than they had expected.

There was quite a bit of enemy fire on the coast, and we were being heavily fired upon as we approached. . . . The lad in front of me was Rifleman Philip Gianelli, and as the ramp went down, he took a burst of machine-gun fire in his stomach, ahead of me, while I wasn't touched by that burst. There was a **tracer** in the burst, and you could see it coming to us, and Gianelli was killed instantly.

I got off the landing craft and crossed the narrow sandy beach to the edge of the beach sand dune. I got some protection, but still, I suffered a piece of **shrapnel** lodged in my right nostril. I was unconscious for some time, and being one of the early waves on the beach, there was no first aid station. . . . Finally there were five or six walking wounded, and we formed up a section and moved off the beach to follow the route of our company inland, and I went to the village of Sainte-Croix, which our battalion had taken. There were a number of dead Germans lying in the streets.

Canadian soldiers waded ashore from landing craft onto Juno Beach. Some soldiers were killed by machine-gun fire before they had even set foot on dry land.

Gaining a Foothold

The **Allies** gradually gained control of Juno, Sword, Gold, and Utah Beaches. The last to be taken was Omaha Beach, one of the two American landing sites. Omaha was expected to be difficult because steep cliffs behind the beach formed a natural wall. Also, it was more heavily defended by Germans than the Allies had anticipated. Aerial bombing from planes and bombardments from offshore ships had failed to damage the German gun stations looking down on the beach. Worse yet, the bad weather turned the waters around Omaha Beach into a heaving mass. U.S. Navy ships launched their landing craft from twelve miles (19 kilometers) out, rather than the planned eight miles (13 kilometers). All of these factors combined to make it almost impossible to capture the beach.

The Germans sensed the Americans' dismay and confusion and believed that they could hold onto the beach. German machine guns opened fire on landing craft as soon as they unloaded their troops. The Allies suffered heavily at Omaha Beach: 2,500 Americans were dead, missing, or wounded by nightfall. The beach was taken only because of the planning before the landing itself. The French **Resistance** and Allied bombing had successfully blocked German supply routes. As no extra ammunition could reach the Germans, they were forced to withdraw.

Grim clouds form a suitable backdrop for the American troops as they wade ashore at Omaha, the most difficult of the five landing beaches to capture.

William Stanley remembers landing at Omaha Beach

Infantryman William J. Stanley was part of the American invasion force that landed on Omaha Beach on the morning of June 6, 1944. His account shows how difficult conditions were at Omaha—even before the men set foot on the beach.

We circled for one and a half hours in the storm, then headed for the beach. One hundred feet [30 meters] from shore, my landing craft hit a sand bar. Thinking we were on the beach, the ramp was dropped, which was a signal to disembark. We ran into twelve feet [3.7 meters] of water. There was widespread panic. The weak and non-swimmers drowned. The war ended for them one hundred feet from the invasion on Omaha Beach. The shock, fear, and reality of what happened is indescribable.

When my feet touched the beach, I made my way to shore, stumbling and pushing bodies of my American comrades aside. There was one way to go—ahead. Gunfire hit the water, and bodies became sandbags and protection. Not one American son could ever be prepared for this. Everything was instinctive and I kept moving ahead.

We huddled behind the sand dunes on the beach while the **artillery** continued firing toward us. The choice was either to huddle there and be killed by gunfire or move forward.

The Grim Struggle

All through the day of June 6, the fighting continued. Mines and underwater explosives ripped some **Allied** landing craft apart even before they reached the shore. German machine-gun nests picked off soldiers almost at will, often concentrating their fire on officers, whom they could recognize by their uniforms. As a result many groups of soldiers, especially on Omaha Beach, found themselves without commanding officers. For them, victory seemed like a distant hope. Simply surviving became the main battle.

Colonel S. A. Marshall, landing with the American forces at Omaha, described what seemed to be a hopeless position as men arrived by landing craft: "The ramp drops. In that instant, two machine guns concentrate their fire on the opening. Not a man is given time to jump. All aboard are cut down where they stand."

Even so, by nightfall, it had become clear that the main objective of the D-Day operation—taking the five beaches—had succeeded. The cost had been great, though, and it was not yet clear whether the Germans would be pushed back from their stronghold in Normandy.

Armed Allied guards stand watch over the thousands of German soldiers who were captured during the fighting of June 6, 1944.

Ernie Pyle reports

Ernie Pyle was one of the most respected and best-loved of America's war reporters. He joined the American forces in Normandy one day after the D-Day landings. His first report paints a vivid picture of a grim and bloody battlefield.

By the time we got here the beaches had been taken and the fighting had moved a couple of miles inland. All that remained on the beach was some sniping and **artillery** fire, and the occasional startling blast of a mine geysering [spewing] brown sand into the air. That plus a gigantic and pitiful litter of wreckage along miles of shoreline.

Submerged tanks and overturned boats and burned trucks and shell-shattered jeeps and sad little personal belongings were strewn all over these bitter sands. That plus the bodies of soldiers lying in rows covered with blankets, the toes of their shoes sticking up in a line as though on drill. And other bodies, uncollected, still sprawling grotesquely in the sand or half hidden by the high grass beyond the beach.

That, plus an intense, grim determination of work-weary men to get this chaotic beach organized and get all the vital supplies and the reinforcements moving more rapidly over it from the stacked-up ships standing in droves out to sea.

Soldiers of Color

By nightfall on June 6, 1944, all five landing beaches had been captured by the **Allies.** British and American ships set up floating docks offshore to make it easier to unload more troops and equipment. The great drive to free Europe from German domination had begun, but months of fierce fighting still lay ahead.

Among the many American troops now on French soil were several African-American units. Many of these soldiers came from areas of the United States where they faced **discrimination** and inequality. Given the chance to defend basic freedoms against **Nazi oppression,** however, these men fought bravely alongside other Allied troops. Their bravery and loyalty to America showed the falseness of those Americans who would deny African Americans their basic rights at home. The experience also gave African Americans more confidence to demand those same basic rights in the decades after the war.

Despite recognition on the battlefield, however, the U.S. armed forces did not start an integration process until the 1950s.

Black soldiers from countries such as the United States, Tunisia, and Guyana played an important part in the D-Day landings. Here, African-American soldiers unload ammunition for the Allied soldiers. This dangerous work was often done under German machine-gun fire.

"I don't know how we did it"

African-American newspapers were the only way that many could learn about the contribution of African Americans to the war. This is an excerpt from an article by Ollie Stewart in *The Afro-American,* written just after D-Day, about African-American efforts in the first days after the landings.

Leaving from England, [African-American] soldiers loaded us on a boat, others accompanied us over, and still others unloaded us and much equipment on the beach they helped win from the enemy during the first few days of the invasion. . . . All last night, guns shook the ground on which I slept. Our Long Toms slugged it out with German 88's in a duel that has no end.

Private Warren Capers and others from his unit set up a medical station that aided 300 soldiers on D-Day. Capers was recommended for a **Silver Star** for his bravery.

I am staying with a quartermaster outfit [which] has five **purple hearts** for wounds resulting from enemy action. . . . Another unit has among its personnel Cpl. John Hawkins of Pine Bluff, Arkansas, who shot down a German plane on D-Day while landing under fire with a trucking company. Hawkins used a 50-caliber machine gun mounted on the truck to down the raider, which was attempting to strafe [shoot] a troop concentration. The Nazi pilot bailed out and was later captured. . . .

Everywhere I go are tales of our lads who waded ashore in water up to their necks, with their trucks waterproofed, to take part in the assault that forced Jerry [Allied slang for a German soldier] from his strong points. Many are still saying, "I don't know how we did it, after seeing how Jerry was dug in."

French Reaction

France had been defeated by Germany in the middle of 1940. The parts of the country that were nearest Great Britain—and therefore the likeliest spots for an **Allied** invasion—were ruled directly by the Germans. Most French people living under this German occupation longed for the day when they would once more be able to govern themselves. Many French people joined the **Resistance,** the movement dedicated to helping to free their country from **Nazi** rule.

Their contribution was vital to the success of the D-Day operation. Others, under General Charles de Gaulle, formed the Free French Army, which fought alongside other Allied forces.

On the evening of June 5, a poem by the French poet Paul Verlaine was broadcast on Britain's French radio service. It was a signal to the Resistance that the invasion was under way and their planned **sabotage** attacks could begin. Once the invasion force had landed, Resistance members used their knowledge of the local countryside to help ensure Allied success.

French resistance fighters, some of them women, planned and implemented many sabotage attacks on German communication lines as the Allied invasion force was approaching the Normandy beaches. Here, they are involved in liberating Paris a few months after the D-Day landings.

Many ordinary French people also welcomed the invasion force, providing food and drink to the soldiers who were **liberating** their country. Most knew that the destruction and conflict taking place all around them would lead to German defeat, and they were proud to play their part in the struggle. Others, particularly those who had lost their homes and farms or who saw their home town or city destroyed by the allied bombing, were less overjoyed.

Mademoiselle Genget's diary

Mademoiselle Genget lived in the village of Saint-Come-de-Fresne, near the D-Day invasion beach code-named Gold. Her diary entry on June 6, 1944, reflects her joy and excitement as it becomes clear that the long-awaited invasion has taken place on her own doorstep.

What seemed impossible has really happened! The English have landed on the French coast and our little village has become famous in a few hours! Not one **civilian** killed or wounded. How can we express our surprise after such long years of waiting in wonderment and fear? . . .

What a sight met our eyes [from a nearby cliff]! As far as we could see there were ships of all kinds and sizes and above floated big balloons silvery in the sun. Big bombers were passing and re-passing in the sky. As far as Courseulles [further along the coast] one could see nothing but ships.

Is it all really true? We are at last liberated. The enormous strength that all this war represents is fantastic, and the way it has been handled with such precision is marvellous. . . . A group of Tommies [nickname for the British soldiers] pass and ask us for water. We fill their bottles, say a few words, and, having given chocolates and sweets to the children, they continue on their way.

les
RANC-TIREURS et PARTISANS FRANÇAIS

ONT VERSÉ LEUR SANG

FTP

pour le

DANIEL

PEUPLE de PARIS

This August 1944 poster celebrated the work of the French Resistance. The words announce that members of the Resistance poured out their blood for the people of Paris.

D-Day Plus

Each day after the landings was known as "Day-Day plus 1," "D-Day plus 2," and so forth. On June 11, just a few days after the landings, Hitler issued the order that there was to be no retreat and German soldiers were forced to continue fighting against this massive **Allied** attack. By D-Day plus 23, the Allies had not advanced far into France, although there were 850,000 Allied troops and 150,000 vehicles ashore in Normandy. The German defense still made it hard for the two main groups of Allies—British/Canadian and American—to join forces.

British troops concentrated on the heavily defended city of Caen near Juno, Gold, and Sword Beaches (map page 30). At the end of June, in an attack code-named Operation Epsom, a large-scale Allied **infantry** force attacked west of Caen. It was unsuccessful and resulted in 4,000 men being killed or wounded. Then, General Montgomery, commander-in-chief of the British forces, began Operation Goodwood, designed to take on German forces in a large tank battle to the east of Caen. Despite heavy bombing by Allied planes, Operation Goodwood showed no sign of succeeding even by mid-July. The prolonged British struggle near Caen did, however, begin to have an effect. The Germans were using up precious troops and equipment. With German tanks caught up in the fighting around Caen, the American forces found it easier to capture the important port of Cherbourg.

Lieutenant John Brown's experiences

Lieutenant John Brown, from the British infantry, describes an Allied bombing raid on Caen on July 7, 1944, in the middle of Operation Goodwood. The attack, however, did little to dislodge the Germans from their strongholds in and around the city.

As we lay close up by the start line, we were heartened by the sight of 500 heavy bombers streaming in from the coast in a long unswerving line straight over the city. They completely ignored the heavy **flak** and we watched the bombs come streaming down. One aircraft disappeared completely in a huge white flash, another tilted over and spun down, losing a wing on its journey, but a third, obviously in trouble, flew lower and lower in a large circle, and as it passed over us I could see that all the fabric covering the tail and rudder had been shot away. We marvelled at how it kept on flying, and eventually it appeared to come down well behind our lines. Soon, the whole target area became obscured by smoke and dust, rising high in the air. But still the bombers roared across. This was a terrific **morale** booster for us, but had little effect on our immediate objective, the village of La Bijude, which was well outside the target area.

Normandy was a region of narrow lanes and patchwork fields bounded by earth banks topped with hedges. This hedgerow country proved to be a great defense aid to the Germans. In this picture, British troops shelter from German field-gun fire during the bitter struggle to capture the French city of Caen.

The Battle of Normandy

Throughout July, the **Allies** slowly began to make progress against the Germans in what became known as the Battle of Normandy. Hitler, still convinced that a larger Allied invasion was yet to come in northern France, refused to send essential supplies and troops south. The British finally captured the city of Caen, though there was little of it left standing after the heavy Allied bombing. Cherbourg and the inland town of Saint-Lô were already in Allied hands. Now the Allies controlled all of the Normandy Peninsula, from Caen in the north to Avranches in the south (map page 30). It was time now to break out and move eastward against German troops in the rest of France.

American General Omar Bradley began the breakout on July 25 with an attack south from Saint-Lô. British and Canadian troops moved south and east from Caen. About a week later, another American attack moved east from Avranches. The Germans were in retreat but put up a last valiant effort near the town of Falaise. They held out until August 20, and then retreated across the Seine River. The retreat allowed Allied troops, along with members of the French **Resistance** and Free French troops, to **liberate** Paris on August 25.

The Normandy town of Saint-Lô, which blocked the Allied advance from the landing beaches, lies in ruins after weeks of heavy fighting.

Major-General Meyer remembers

Major-General Kurt Meyer had led his German troops from Caen to Falaise in late July 1944. They were part of Germany's last attempt to stop the Allied advance. Here he describes the fighting on August 14 and 15, 1944, around some high ground given the name Hill 159 by the German army. In September, Meyer was captured and handed over to the Americans.

We do not understand the enemy. . . . His vastly superior numbers of tanks only have to drive over us at full speed to finish us, but nothing happens. Each attack is repulsed until the afternoon. . . . Fighter bombers launch themselves on the little forest of Bois du Roi unleashing their rockets into the long destroyed forest. Some tanks east of Hill 159 fall victim to the Typhoon [fighter plane armed with bombs or rockets] attacks. I meet Max Wünsche [a comrade], between Versainville and Hill 159. He tells me of the now hopeless situation on the hill. Enemy tanks race toward us. Their shells explode on the road, Max Wünsche disappears. I feel a burning hot pain, blood runs across my face, I dive head first into a little hedge, a shell splinter has cut my head open. I look dizzily at the road. Our Kubelwagen [open-topped tank] has disappeared and Max Bornhöft [another comrade] is no longer to be seen. I am alone, but at no time do I feel deserted. I know my comrades will not leave me here.

What Have We Learned from D-Day?

The D-Day landings of June 6, 1944, were the largest invasion in history. The **Allied** military leaders planned every aspect of the operation and practiced it over and over in the months leading up to Operation Overlord. Soldiers from all over the world were involved. Even though things did not always go according to plan, a spirit of determination and cooperation meant that the operation succeeded despite bad weather and fierce German resistance. Some people have argued that mistakes were made after the five beaches were captured. The grim battles that followed were made worse by a lack of coordination among those directing the troops and the confusion of the soldiers during battle. But on both sides, the fighting was very fierce. The German troops knew they were fighting for their survival, while Allied troops felt they were fighting for their freedom and the freedom of Europe.

The lessons of this great battle go far beyond providing guidelines for future military operations. Everyone on the Allied side felt that they could play a part in preserving freedom, even if it was the soldiers who might pay the ultimate price—death. (Roughly 150,000 soldiers, sailors, and airmen lost their lives in the Normandy campaign.) The planning, efforts, and sacrifices of D-Day were crucial and paved the way for the Allied victory in Europe in May 1945. Although D-Day was terribly costly in terms of death and destruction, there appeared to be no other way of **liberating** Europe from **Nazi** aggression.

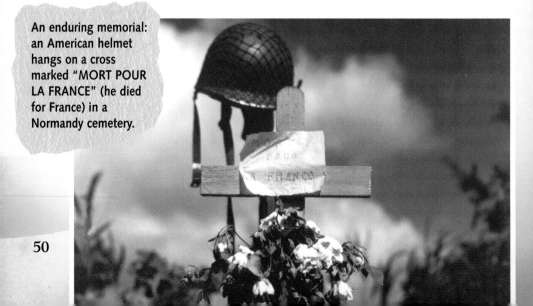

An enduring memorial: an American helmet hangs on a cross marked "MORT POUR LA FRANCE" (he died for France) in a Normandy cemetery.

Stephen Ambrose remembers how ordinary people felt about D-Day

The American historian Stephen Ambrose, who died in October 2002, was one of the leading experts on D-Day and World War II in general. Here, he looks back to his own experiences at the time of D-Day.

One of the features of D-Day is, we were all involved. I was making the contribution that a 10-year-old could make; my mother was making the contribution she could make. Women all over this country were working night shifts in the factories, turning out **munitions** or boots or binoculars or any of the other many items that troops need to go into battle. And then they were working days, volunteers at the Red Cross rolling bandages. When the news came to this country on the morning of June 6 that the invasion had started, there was an overwhelming impulse to go to church or synagogue and pray, and what these people prayed was, "God, I hope I did it right. The bandages that I rolled, the bullets that I made are going into battle, even as I am here praying. Please, God, let me have done it right."

Timeline

1939   September 1: Germany invades Poland, triggering the start of World War II in Europe.

1940   May 10: Germany invades Belgium and the Netherlands. Winston Churchill becomes the new British prime minister.

        June 22: Germany's victory over France is complete.

1941   June 22: Germany invades the **Soviet Union.**

        December 7: Japan attacks Pearl Harbor on the island of Oahu in Hawaii.

        December 11: Germany and Italy declare war on the United States.

1942   October 23: General Montgomery wins a victory against the Germans at El Alamein in Egypt, North Africa. Eisenhower leads the **Allied** forces in Operation Torch in North Africa.

1943   May 12–25: British Prime Minister Winston Churchill meets President Franklin Roosevelt in Washington, D.C., to discuss the cross-channel invasion called D-Day.

        September 3: Italy secretly surrenders to the Allies, but Germany controls most of the country.

        September 9: Allied troops land at Salerno, Italy.

        December 24–29 : Announcements in London and Washington, D.C., reveal that General Dwight Eisenhower is to be the Supreme Allied Commander for the D-Day invasion. Admiral Sir Bertram Ramsay and Air Marshal Leigh Mallory will lead the air and naval forces.

1944   June 6—D-Day: Allied troops land in Normandy to begin the invasion in northern France.

Below are the approximate times and sequence of the events of D-Day:

00:00: First airborne troops begin to land.

01:00: Landing craft begin to be lowered into the water; **paratroopers** cut phone lines and knock down telephone poles.

02:00: First bombers take off to attack targets around the beachhead.

03:00: Gliders begin to reinforce paratroopers.

03:09: German radar detects Allied invasion fleet. Admiral Krancke orders shore defenses to prepare for invasion.

05:20: Bombers drop first bombs on German targets at sunrise.

05:35: German **artillery** opens fire; Allied naval forces return fire.

06:20: Allied landing craft approach the beaches.

06:30: American troops land at Utah and Omaha Beaches.

07:25: British troops begin to land at Sword Beach.

07:35: British troops land at Gold Beach.

08:00: Canadian troops land at Juno Beach.

08:30: Landing craft begin delivery of armor at Omaha Beach.

10:45: Utah Beach nearly captured; more troops come ashore.

12:00: Gold, Juno, and Sword Beaches under Allied control.

13:00: Troops at Omaha begin to capture the beach.

16:00: Hitler finally gives approval to release **panzers** to combat Allied invasion. It is too late to prevent the success of the Allied landings.

June, July, and August: Battle of Normandy takes place.

August 25: Paris is **liberated** by American and French forces.

Sources for Further Research

Books

Duboscq, Genevieve. *My Longest Night: A Twelve-Year-Old Heroine's Stirring Account of D-Day and After.* New York: Arcade Publishing, 1994.

Green, Robert. *Vive la France: The French Resistance During World War II.* Danbury, Conn.: Scholastic Library Publishing, 1995.

Klam, Julie. *From D-Day to V-E Day.* North Mankato, Minn.: Smart Apple Media, 2002.

Rees, Bob. *The D-Day Landing Sites.* Chicago: Heinemann Library, 2002.

Sheehan, Sean. *D-Day, June 6, 1944.* Chicago: Raintree Publishers, 2002.

Websites

http://www.ibiscom.com/w2frm.htm
Eyewitness accounts of World War II from people who were there. Audio links provide actual newscasts of some of the events.

List of Primary Sources

The author and publisher gratefully acknowledge the following publications and websites from which written sources in the book are drawn. In some cases the wording or sentence structure has been simplified to make the material more appropriate for a school readership.

p. 9 Winston Churchill: www.winstonchurchill.org/ffhmount.htm
p. 11 Dean McCandless: www.thedropzone.org/europe/sicily/mccandless.html
p. 13 Private Gordon Carson: *The Victors: Eisenhower and His Boys: the Men of World War II,* Stephen E. Ambrose (Simon & Schuster, 1998).
p. 15 Tehran statement from Roosevelt, Churchill, and Stalin: www.yale.edu/lawweb/avalon/wwii/tehran.htm
p. 17 Guenther Blumentritt: www. normandy.ed.com/normandy
p. 19 Brenda Webb: www.orcadian.co.uk/features/
p. 21 Alan Moorehead: *Eclipse,* Alan Moorehead (Hamish Hamilton, 1945).
p. 23 General Eisenhower: www.spartacus.schoolnet.co.uk/2wwpatton.htm
p. 25 Major Hans von Luck: www. normandy.ed.com/normandy/pri/Q00204.html
p. 27 General Eisenhower: www.eisenhower.utexas.edu/ssa.htm
p. 29 English housewife: *'44: In Combat on the Western Front from Normandy to the Ardennes,* Charles Whiting (Century, 1984).
p. 31 James Delong: www.normandy.ed.com/normandy
p. 33 Sergeant Thornton: www. normandy.ed.com/normandy
p. 35 Franz Gockel: *Voices of D-Day: The Story of the Allied Invasion Told by Those Who Were There,* Edited by Ronald J. Drez. (Louisiana State University Press, 1994).

p. 37 J. H. Hamilton: *Voices of D-Day: The Story of the Allied Invasion Told by Those Who Were There,* Edited by Ronald J. Drez. (Louisiana State University Press: 1994).

p. 39 William J. Stanley: pearlharbor.military.com/nps_history_oral.html

p. 41 Ernie Pyle: *Ernie's War: The Best of Ernie Pyle's World War II Dispatches,* Edited by David Nichols (Random House, 1986).

p. 43 Private Carlton W. Barrett: http://www.dvrbs.com/110thMedBnTxt10.htm

p. 45 Mlle. Genget: *The Victors: Eisenhower and His Boys: the Men of World War II,* Stephen E. Ambrose (Simon & Schuster, 1998).

p. 47 Lieutenant John Brown www.valourandhorror.com/DB/ISSUE/Liberating–Caen.htm

p. 49 Major-General Kurt Meyers: http://search.eb.com/normandy/pri/Q00208.html

p. 51 Stephen E. Ambrose: www.c-span.org/mmedia/booknote/ lambbook/transcripts/10005.htm

Glossary

alliance   agreement between countries to support one another

Allies   referring to the countries, including Great Britain, France, the U.S., and the Soviet Union, that fought against the Axis powers

amphibious   involving activities in water and on land

antiaircraft   weapon designed to shoot down aircraft

artillery   cannons and other heavy, powerful weapons that cannot be held by one person

Axis   the military forces of, and the alliance between, Germany, Italy, Japan, and the countries that fought with them during World War II

bastion   any place or institution that protects some basic quality, such as freedom

battery   (in military terms) fortress equipped with artillery

bias   judgment that is clouded by personal opinion

bunker   heavily defended place usually set underground or mainly underground

censorship   removing sensitive military information from letters or newspaper reports during a war

civilian   someone who is not part of an army and not directly involved with fighting

commando   soldier who goes on special, and sometimes secret, missions

conscription   required service in the armed forces

convoy   group of ships or other large vehicles traveling together for protection

decryption   decoding of a coded message

discrimination   treating someone unfairly because of race or gender, for example

Eastern Front   part of Eastern Europe, mainly the Soviet Union, where Germany fought against Allied forces

flak   exploding antiaircraft shells

flank   side of a battle area

front   full width of a battle area where two opposing armies meet

garrison   group of troops stationed in a defended place

GI   an abbreviation (widely believed to be "Government Issue") that was used as a nickname for an American soldier

half tide   the point when seawater is halfway between its deepest (high tide) and its shallowest (low tide)

illusory   false and misleading

impregnable   unable to be defeated or destroyed

impulsiveness   acting without thinking about the consequences

indiscretion action that is not based on proper judgment

indoctrinate to fill a person's mind with ideas that he or she cannot criticize

infantry soldiers on foot

intelligence (in military terms) information gained about the enemy

liberate to free someone or something

memoirs personal account of a historical event or period

meteorologist scientist who specializes in studying the weather and how it can be predicted

military dictatorship political structure in which a military leader or leaders have total power to rule the country

minesweeper warship used especially to detect and remove mines laid by the enemy

morale mental state of a person or group of people (whether they are cheerful or confident), usually in times of crisis

Morse code system of dots and dashes representing letters of the alphabet and used to transmit radio messages

munitions weapons and ammunition used in war

Nazi (short for "National Socialist" in German) ruling German political party during World War II

NCO (abbreviation for Non-Commissioned Officer) one of the lowest-ranking officers in the military, such as a corporal or sergeant

opposed landing landing soldiers and equipment along a coastline defended by the enemy

oppressed denied basic rights and freedoms

panzer German tank

paratroopers specially trained soldiers who arrive behind enemy lines by parachute

prejudice belief or opinion formed without a fair examination of the facts

Purple Heart U.S. military decoration awarded to any member of the armed forces wounded or killed in action

reprimand to speak severely to someone because of a wrongdoing

Resistance secret organization of individuals working to overthrow an occupying force

sabotage to destroy or damage something to gain political or military advantage

shrapnel sharp pieces of metal sent flying by an explosion

Silver Star U.S. military decoration awarded to any person who is cited for "gallantry in action" against an enemy of the United States while engaged in military operations involving conflict with an opposing foreign force

Soviet Union (Soviet) communist country that included Russia. It broke into separate countries in the early 1990s.

strategy overall, long-term planning

tracer bullets or artillery shells that are illuminated to help artillery soldiers aim

tyranny uncontrolled use of power by a government or ruler

War Department department of the American government responsible for defense and military actions during World War II; now part of the Department of Defense

Western Front area of military conflict where the Axis powers faced the Allies in Western Europe

Index